In memory of all the things that have ever

been abandoned

•

Objects of everyday use have always been

important representations of culture. Their aesthetic

design often dictates how people treat them.

The object's adoption of human personality traits is

impossible to avoid.

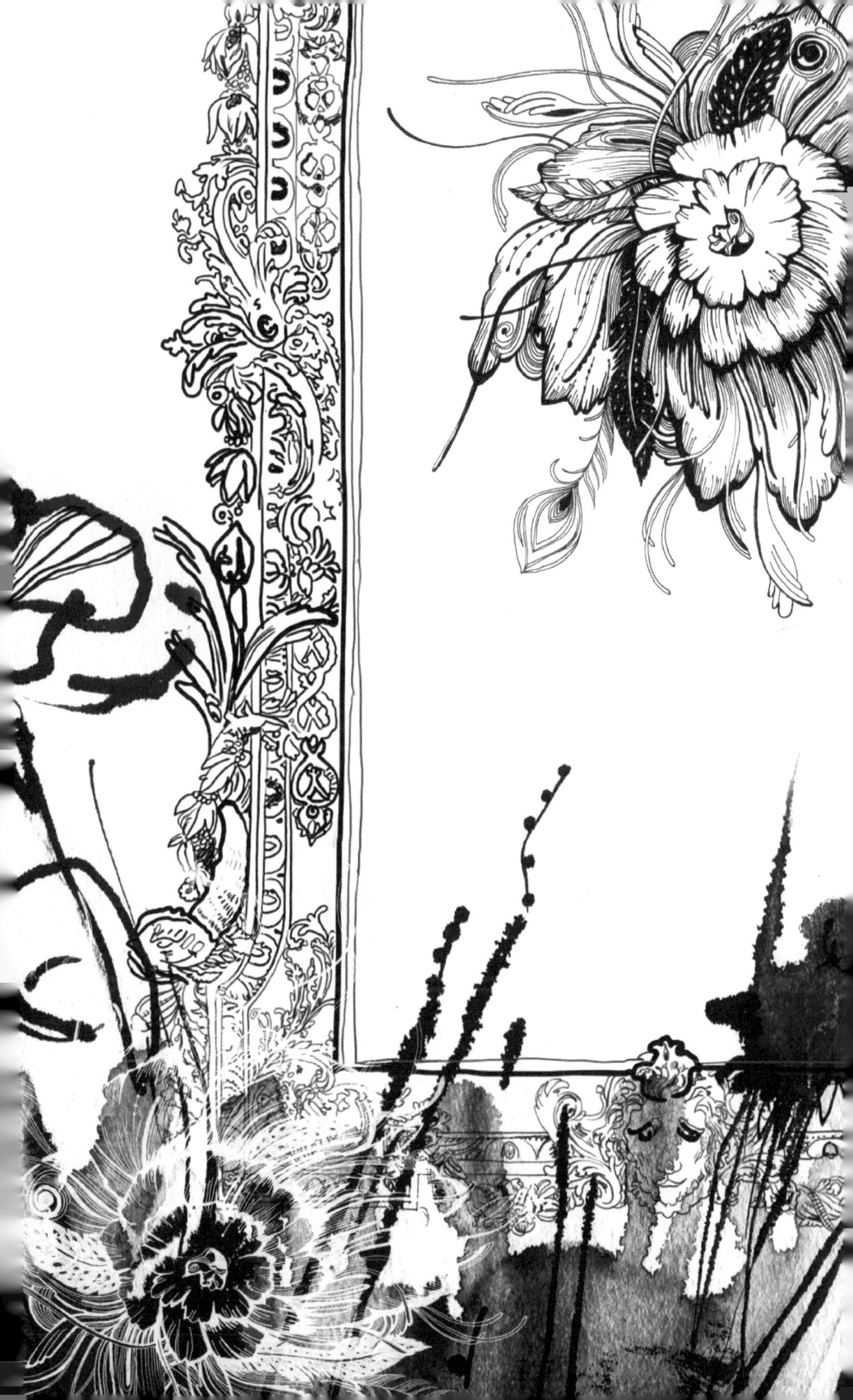

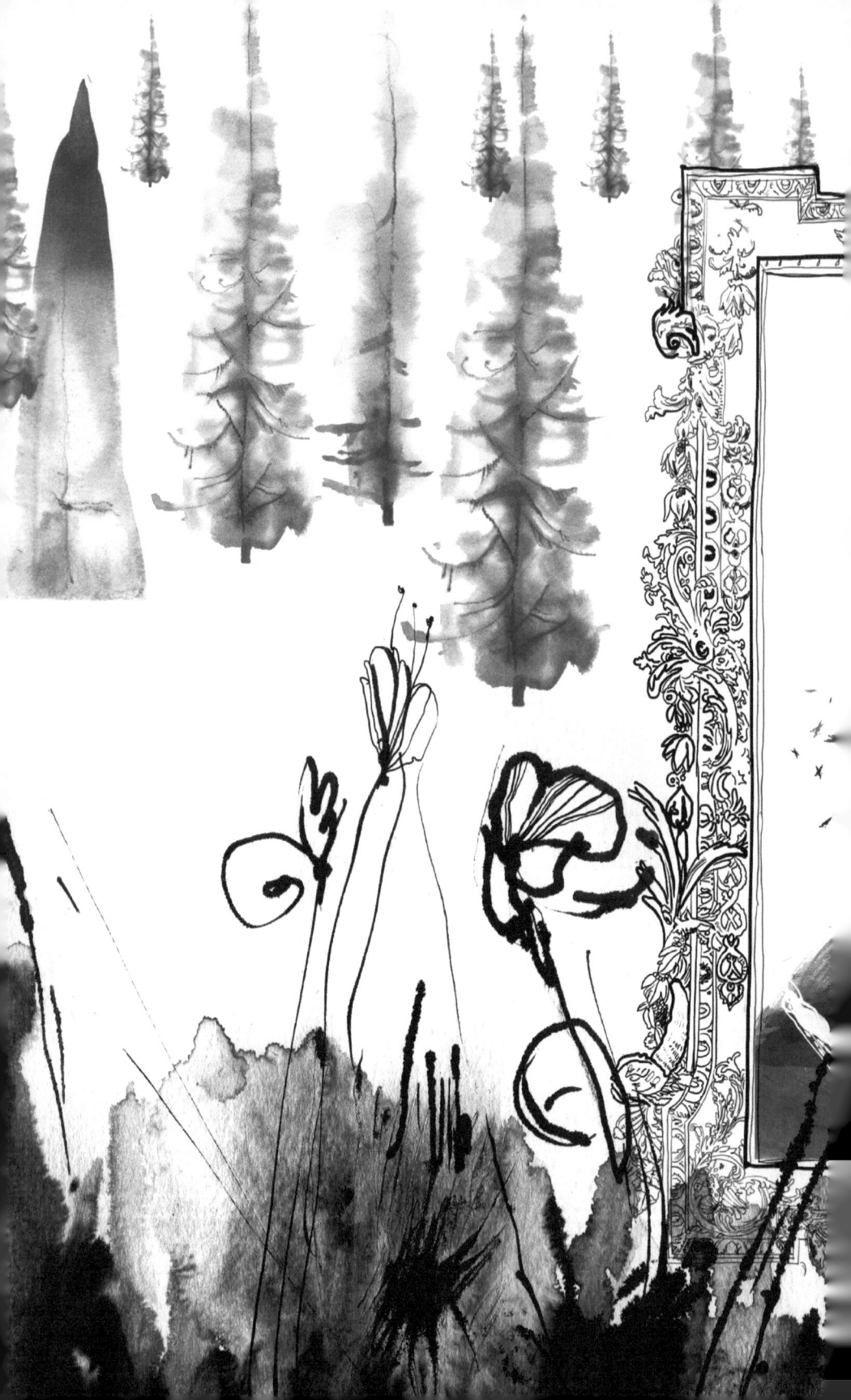

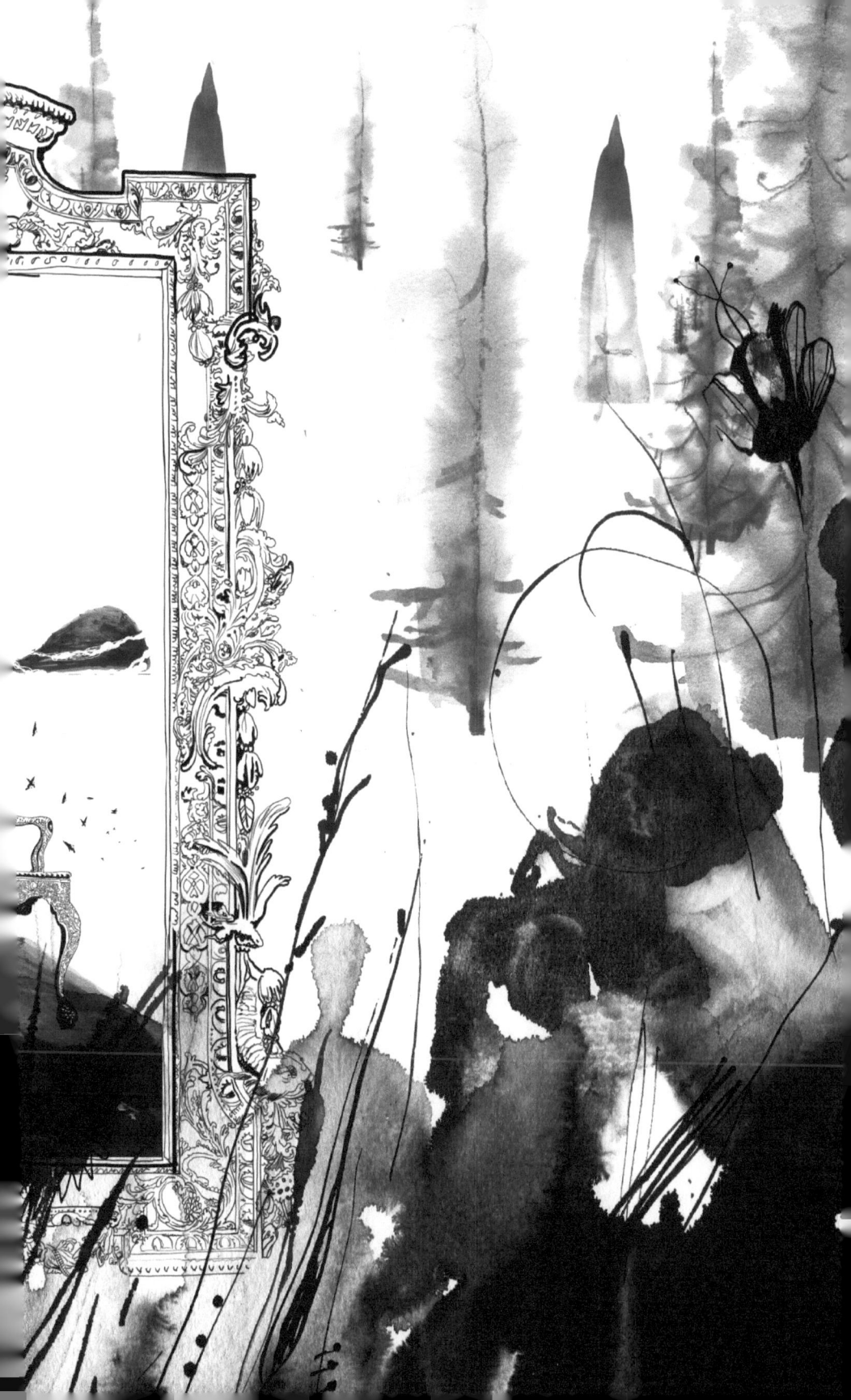

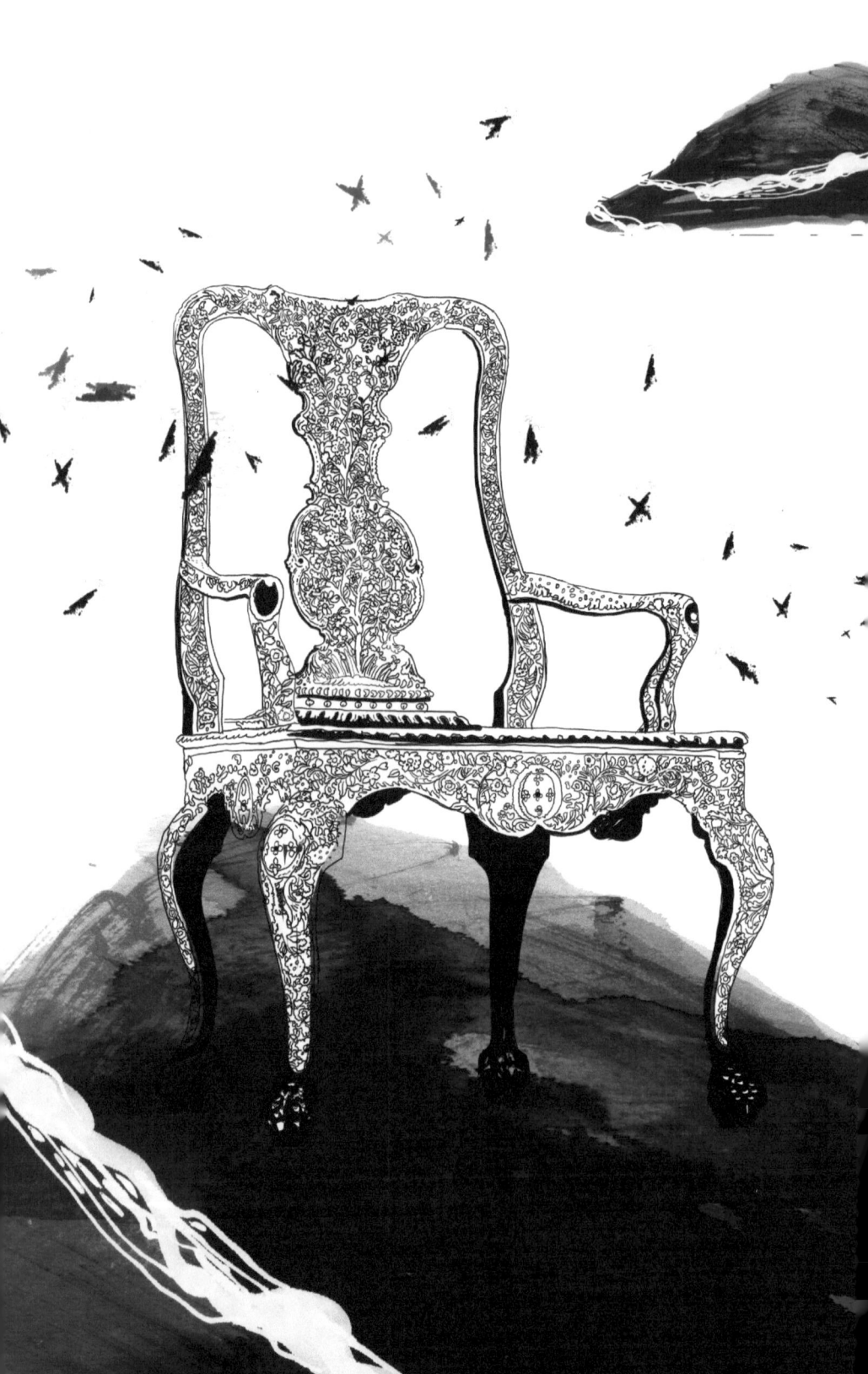

I can't *quite*

remember what happened.

We probably just witnessed

something bad.

The next day the environment around us

had changed.

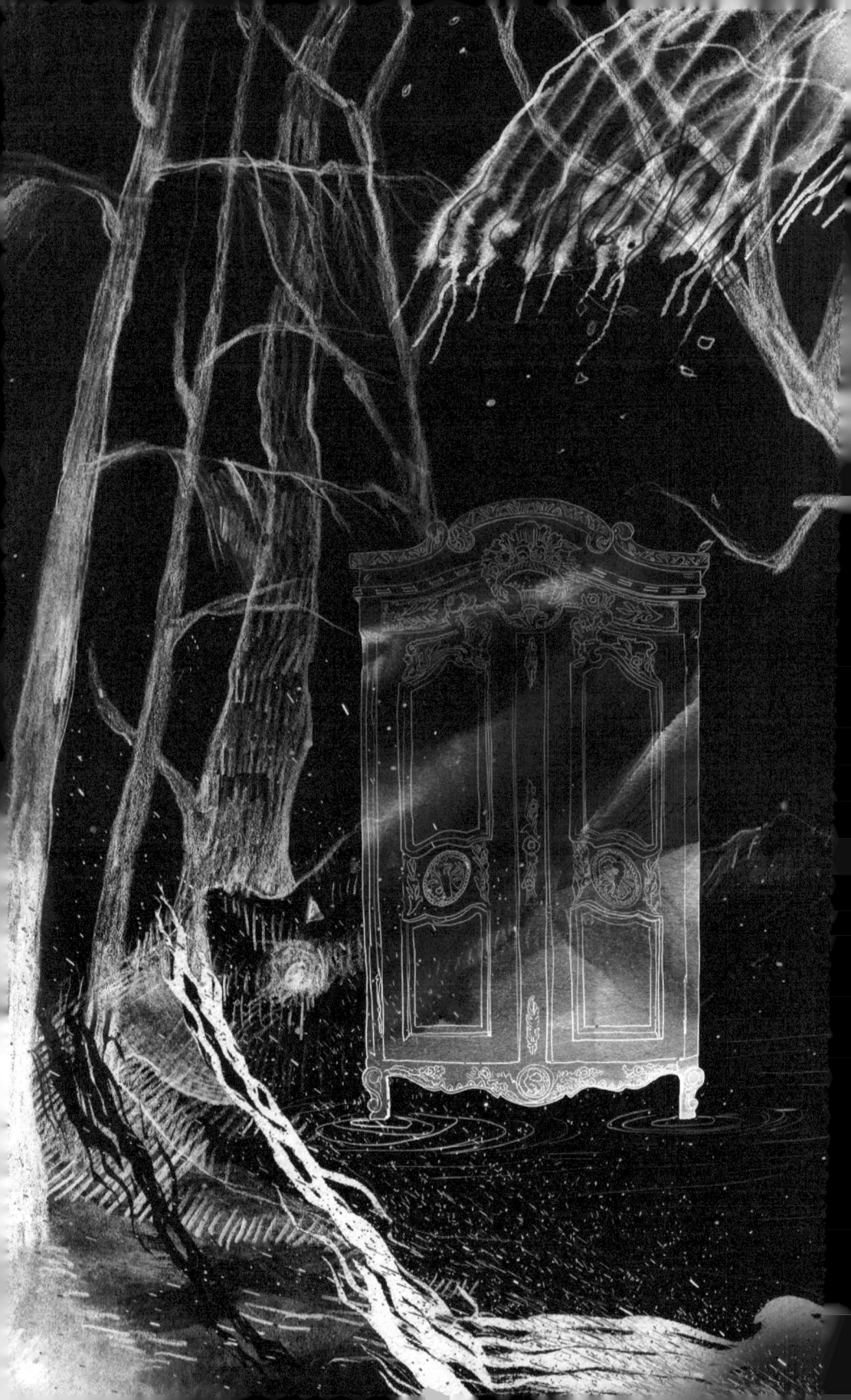

Isn't it *ironic* how we go **back**

to where we came

from?

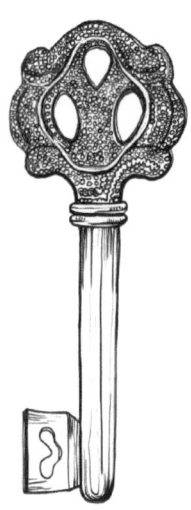

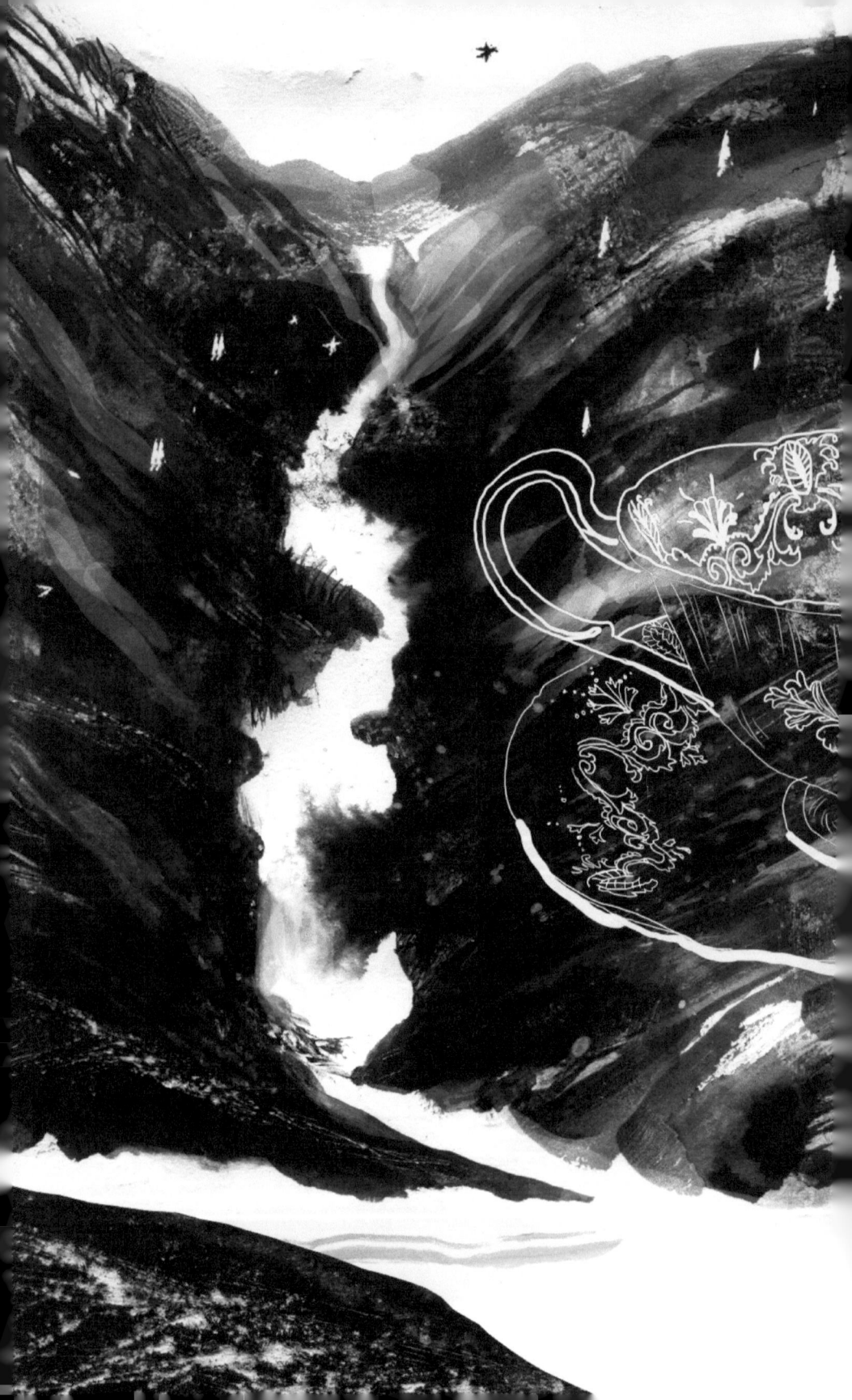

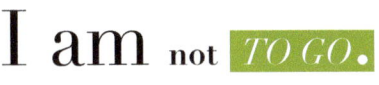

I am not *TO GO.*

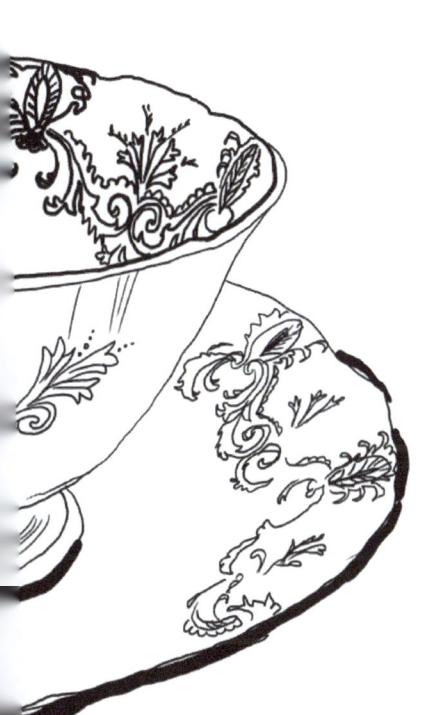

In the **era** of

paper cups

I feel obsolete.

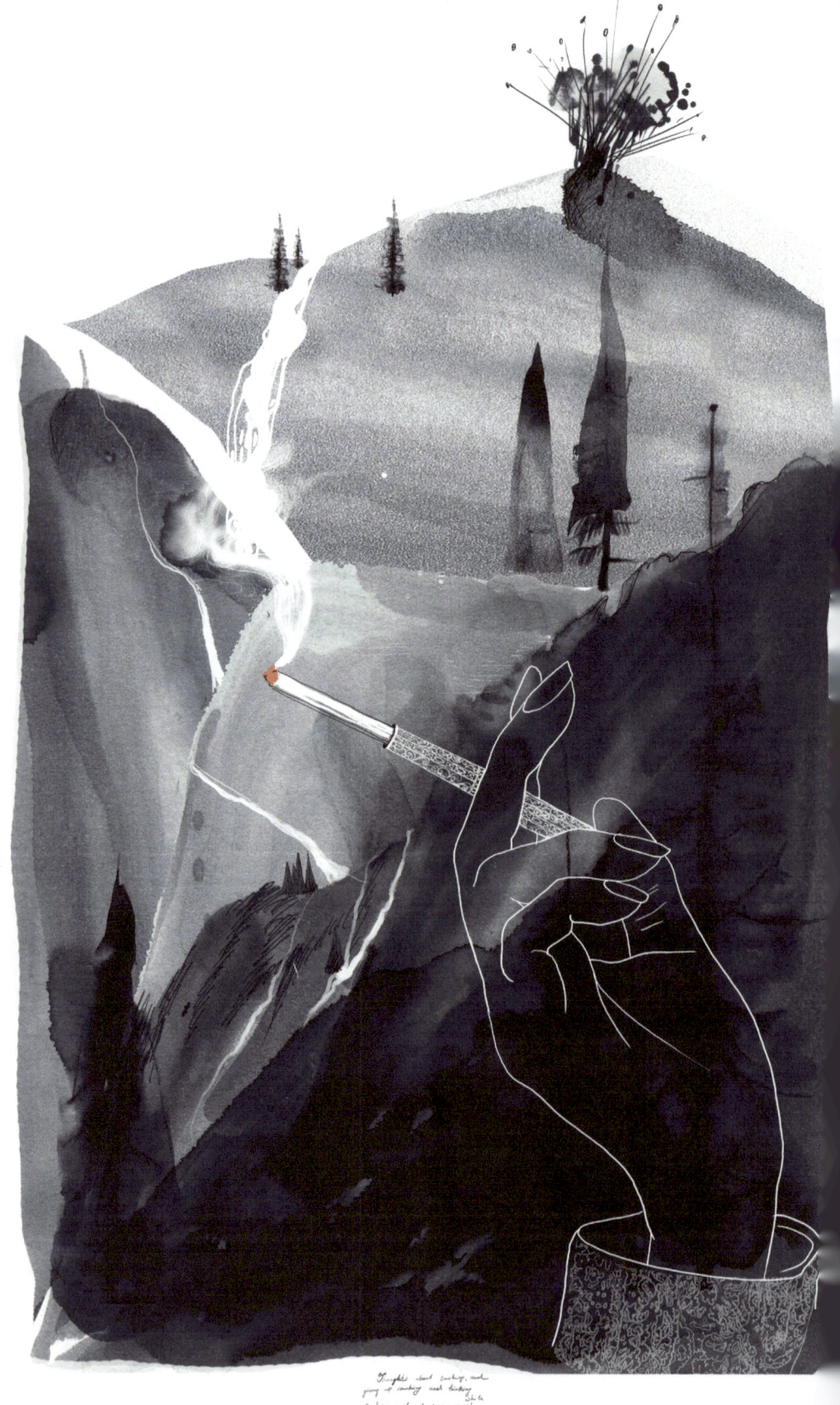

It's

surprising how useless we **became**

when our owners

decided to be **healthy.**

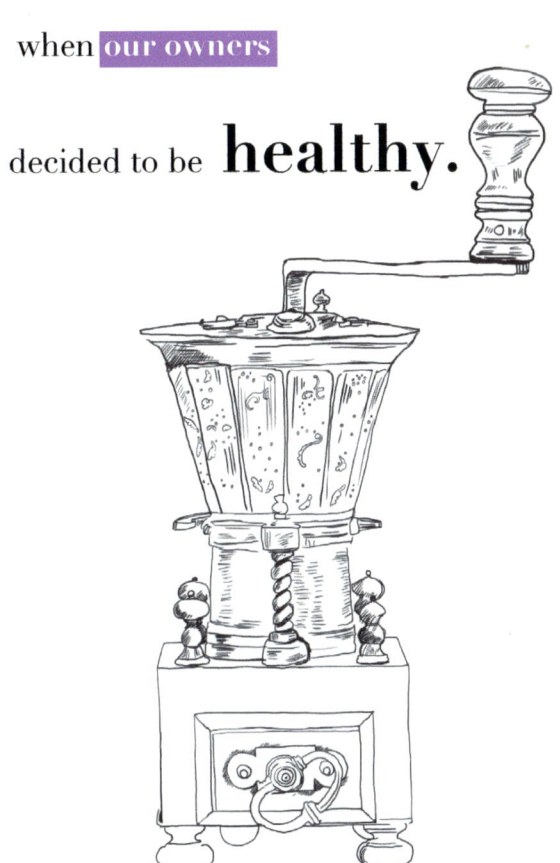

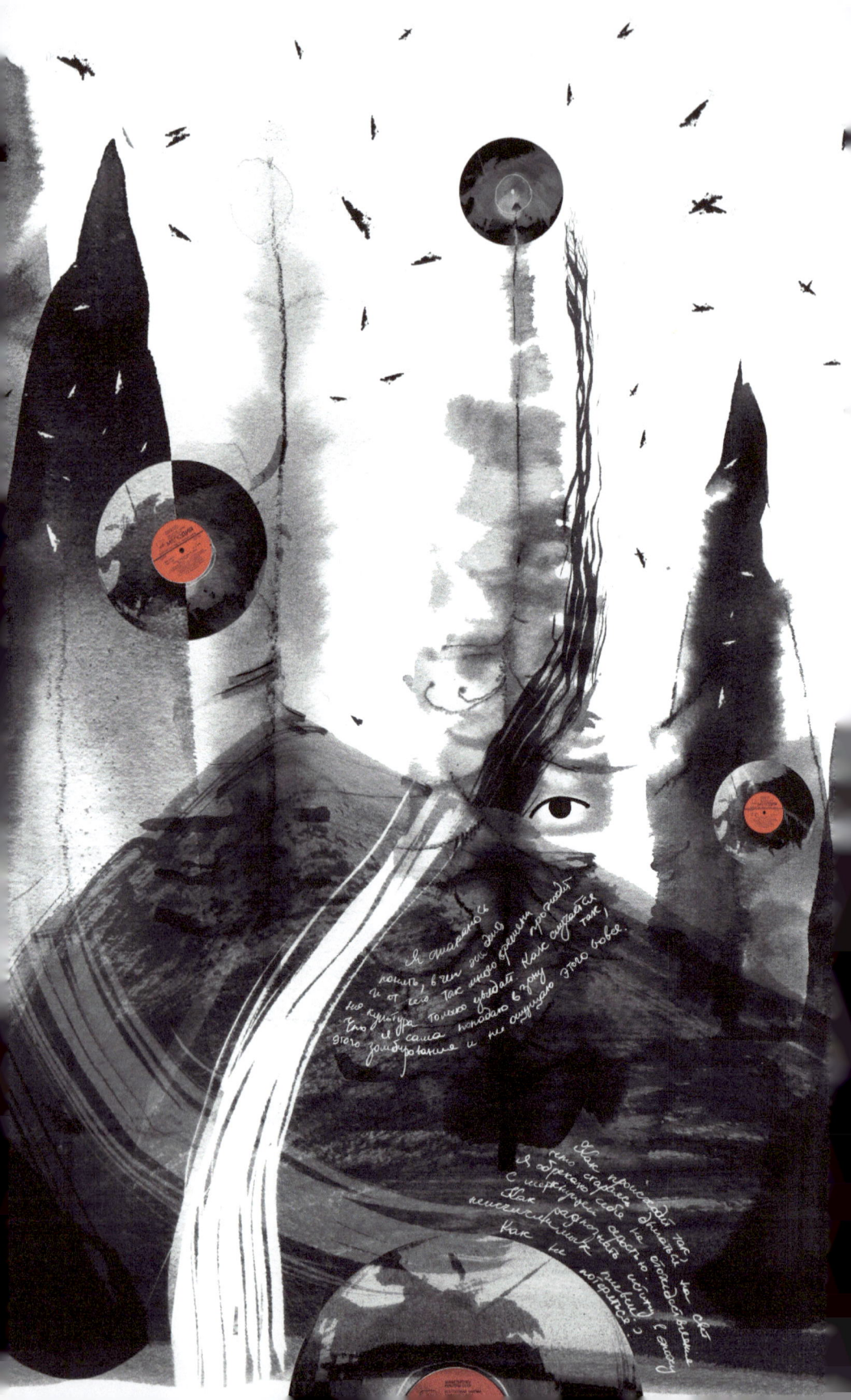

We

would prefer to keep *silent* now

if we can't *sing* properly.

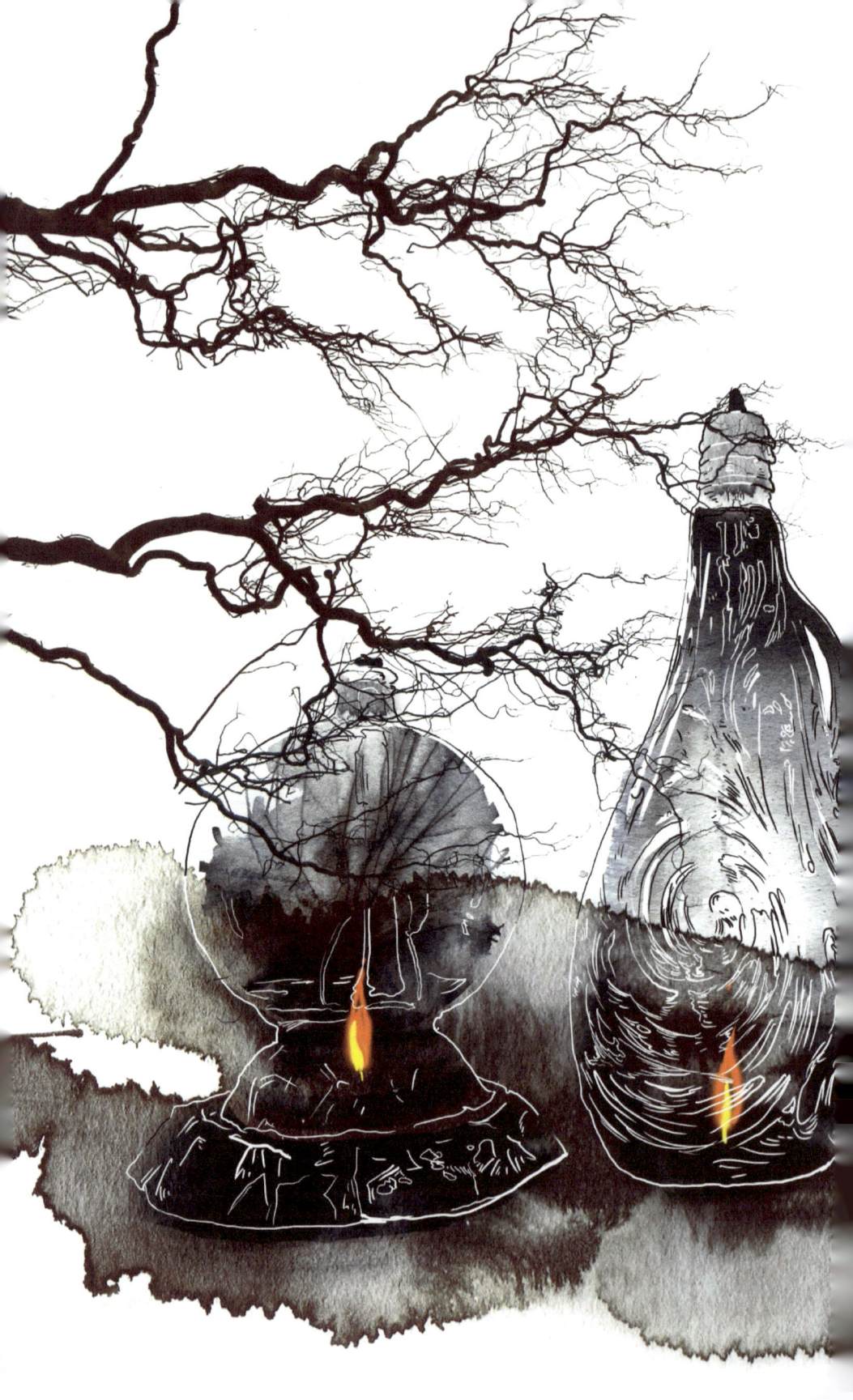

It's **not** *just about*

convenience,

it's about WARMTH.

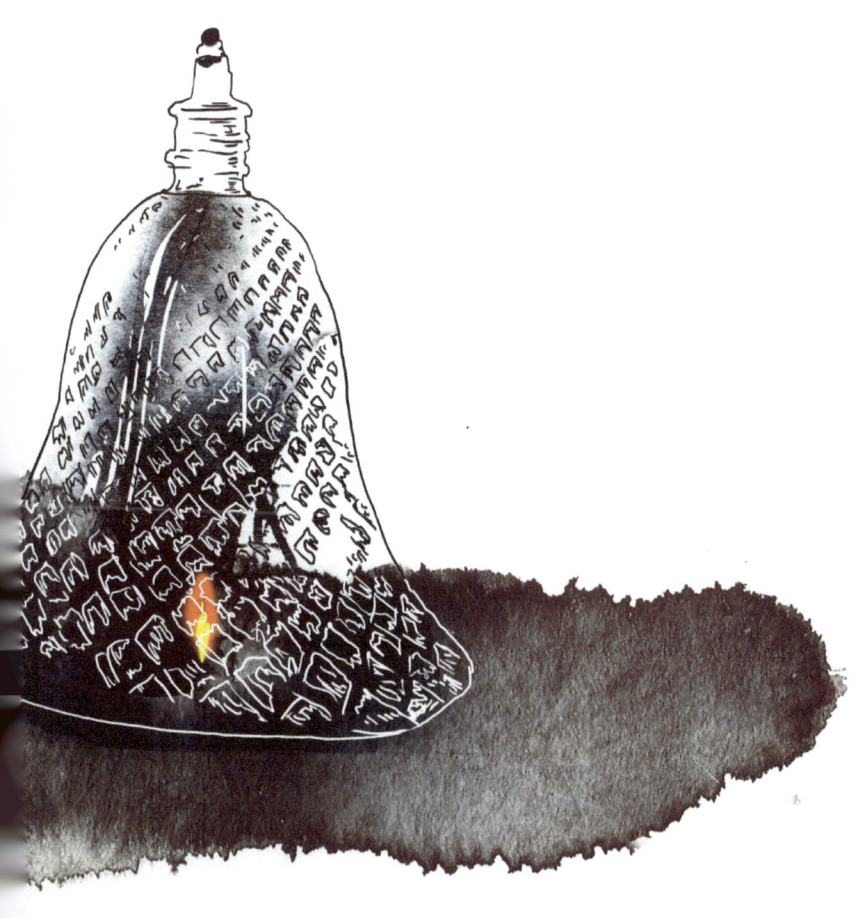

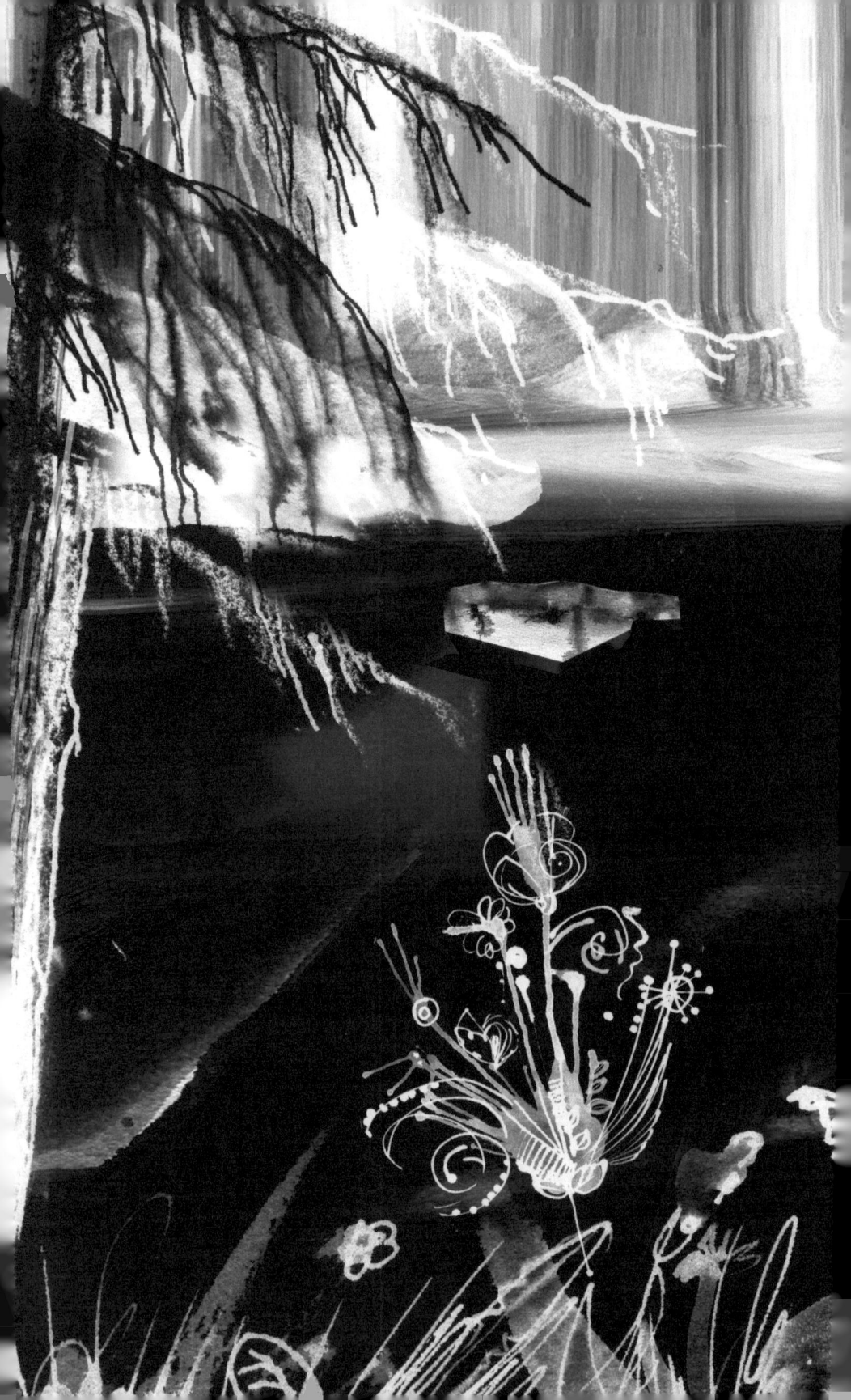

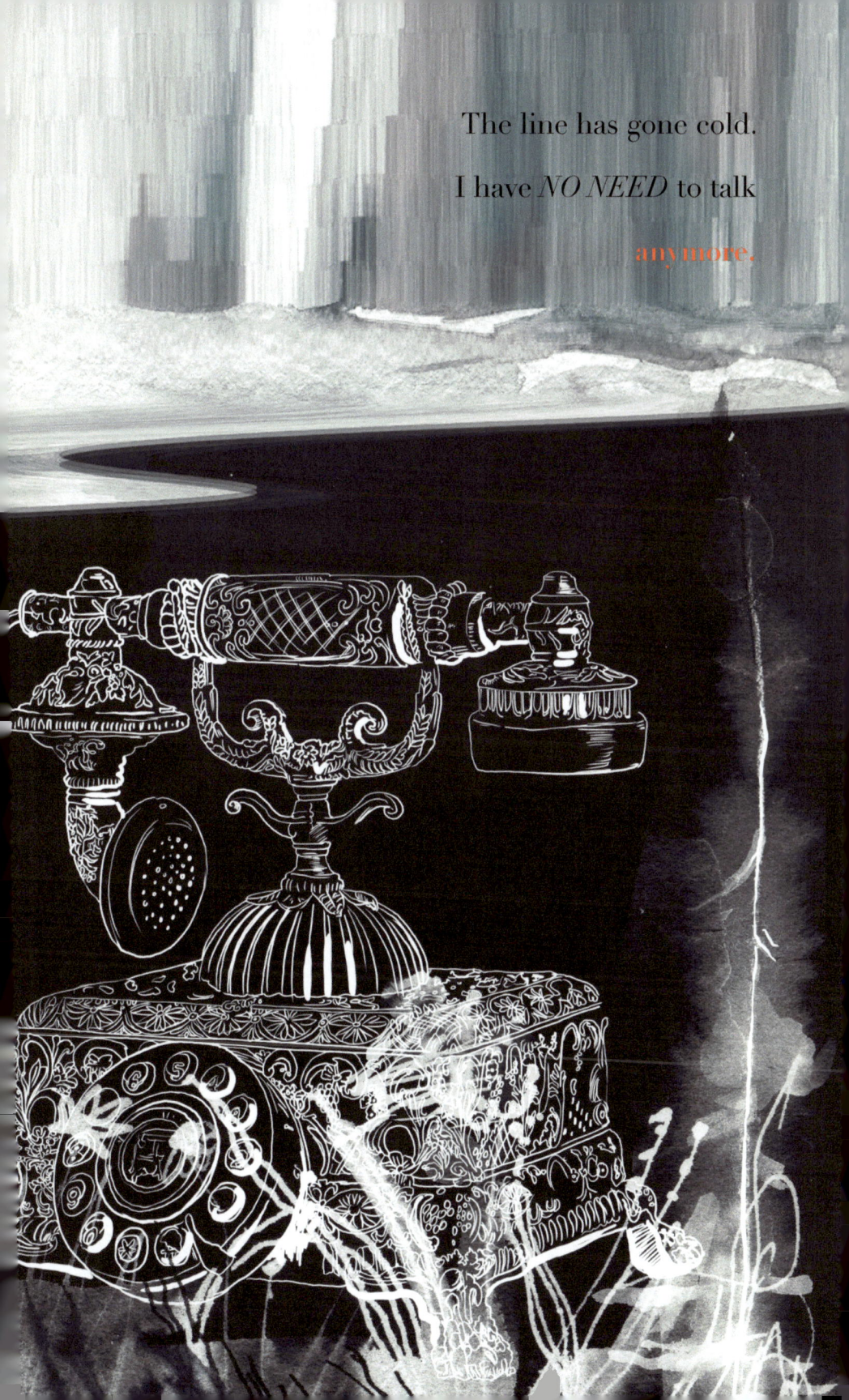

The line has gone cold.

I have *NO NEED* to talk

anymore.

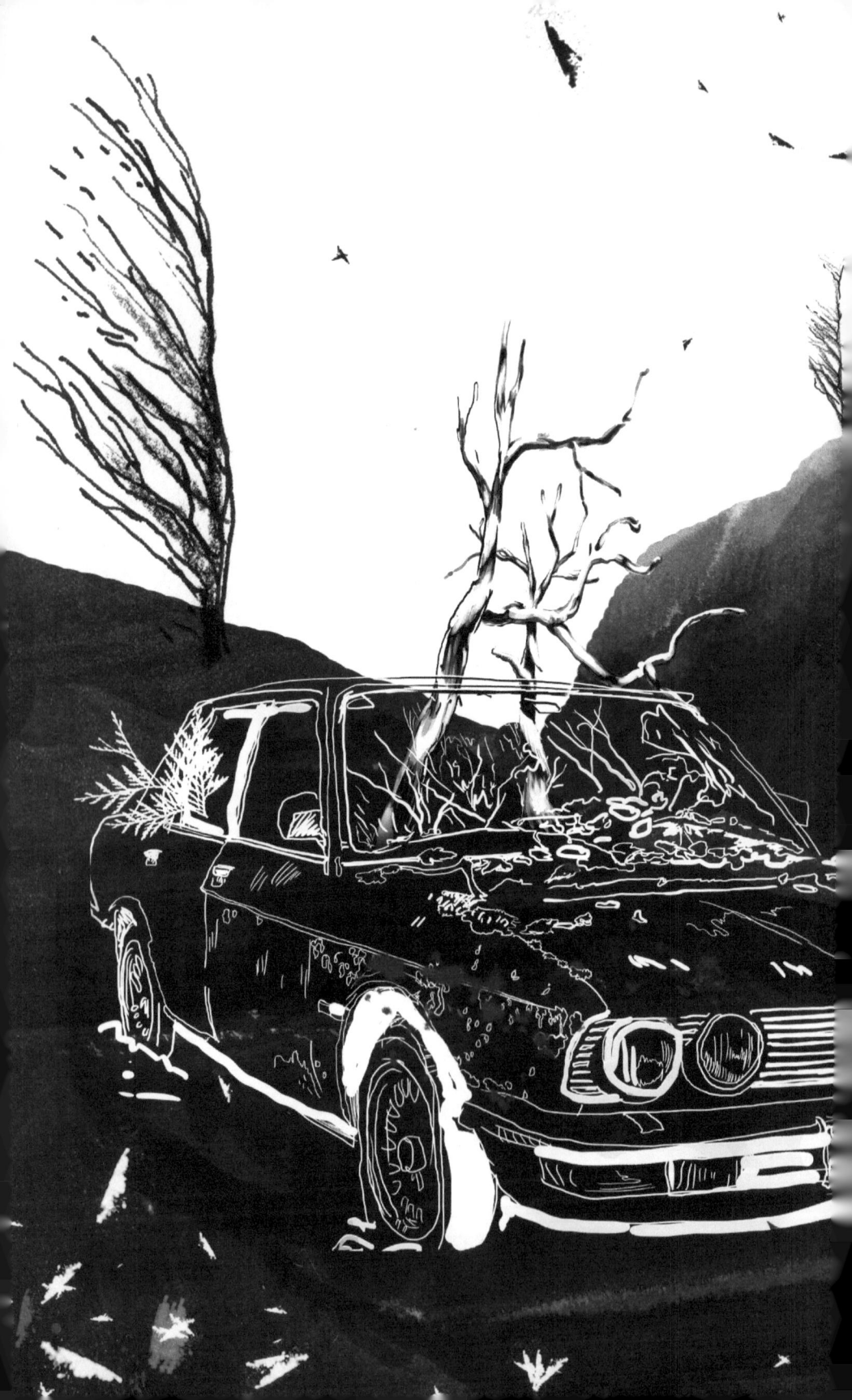

NOTHING *SERVES* FOREVER.

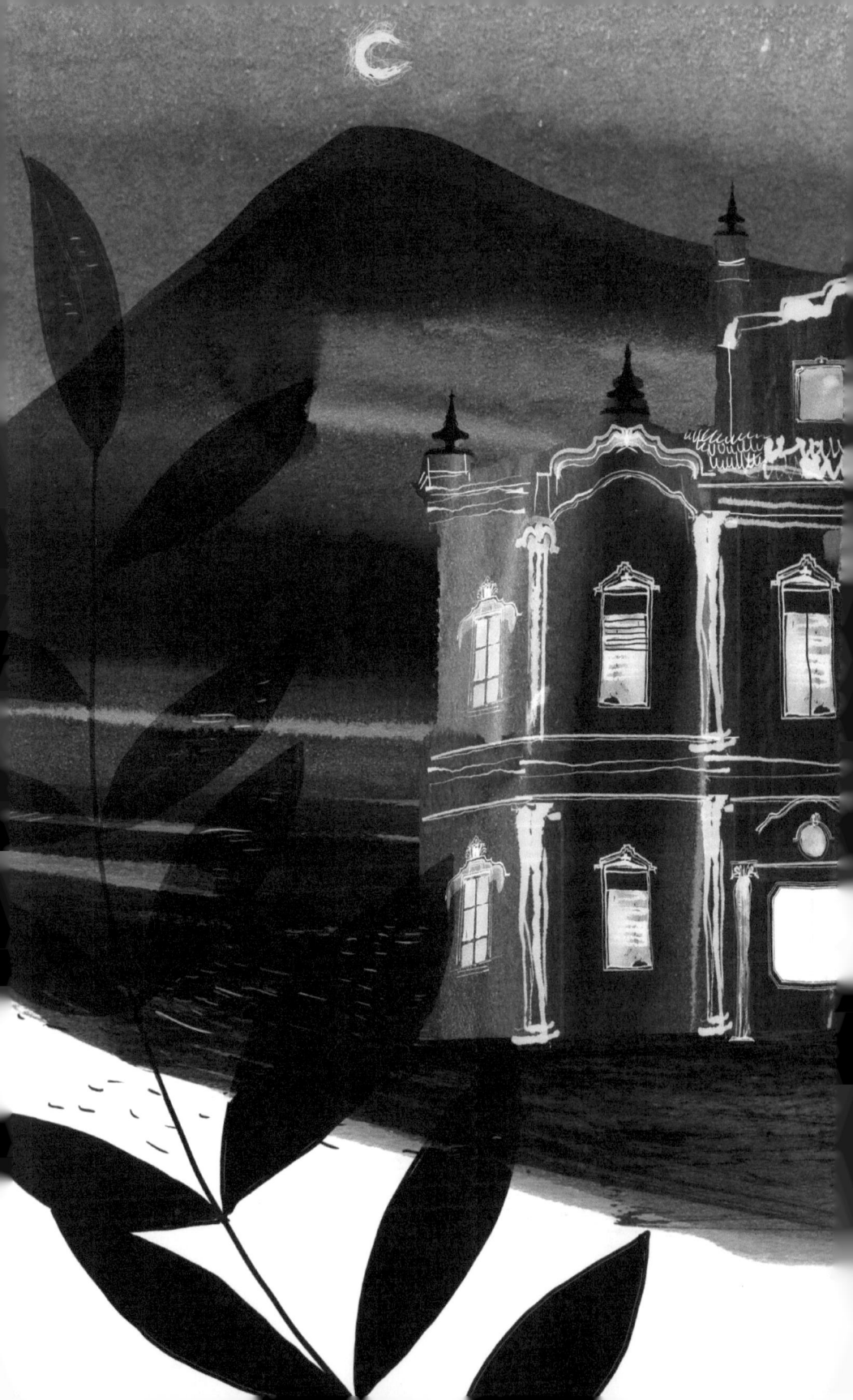

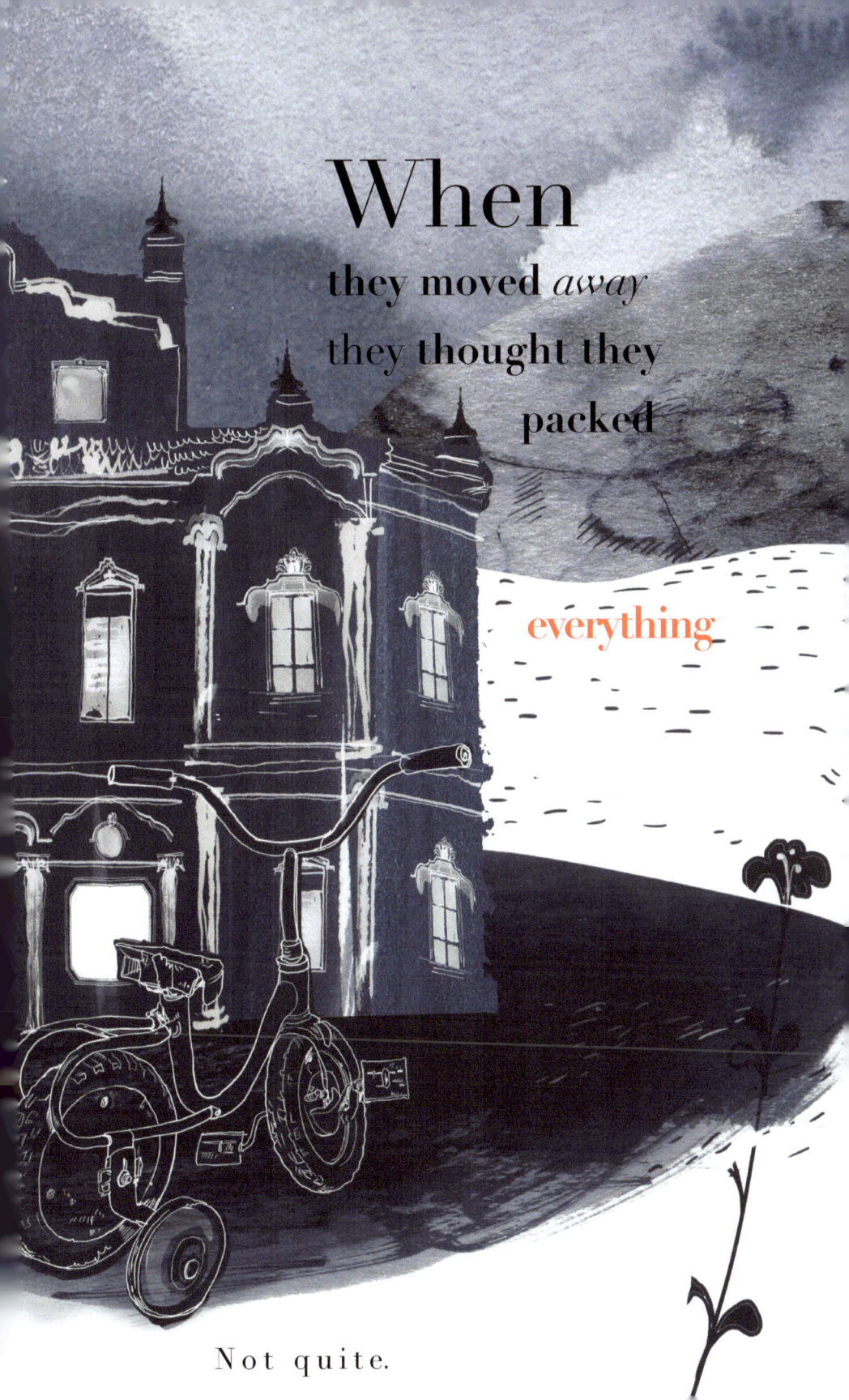

When
they moved *away*
they thought they
packed

everything

Not quite.